In 100 Days or Less

Dr. J. Isaac Vaughn

ISBN-10: 1723015725
ISBN-13: 978-1723015724

DEDICATION

This Book is dedicated to everyone who has a desire to win, but between the win and the process there is a loss of communication. My prayer is that this book opens that conversation back up again. Creating the opportunity for accountability this time. This time you won't have to go at it alone. You will finish In 100 days or Less. Blessings.

CONTENTS

ACKNOWLEDGMENTS

I would like to take this moment to acknowledge a very special group of people for who without them these words may have never been written. To my kids mother, and friend Latissua Barnhardt, my sons Jeremiah, Daniel, and Joshua. This book was written in the worst possible conditions of our lives, we were falling apart, and did fall apart. In that season God taught me that though I had a plan, my plan affected other people besides me, and that it is important to not just have a start and a finish but also consider those who are connected to your dreams. I pray that my mistakes, and my losses are just that, mine. Let these lessons guide you, and these pages fill your heart with God's direction. Even though we are not what you would call a conventional family. We are family and I love each of you. #AlwaysFamily. We Still Win.

1 THE DEVOTIONAL

Every Day Has Meaning and Purpose

"You are the salt of the earth, but if salt has lost its taste, how shall its saltiness be restored? It is no longer good for anything except to be thrown out and trampled under people's feet. "You are the light of the world. A city set on a hill cannot be hidden. Nor do people light a lamp and put it under a basket, but on a stand, and it gives light to all in the house. In the same way, let your light shine before others, so that they may see your good works and give glory to your Father who is in heaven. **Matthew 5:13-16 ESV**

"Agree with God, and be at peace; thereby good will come to you." **Job 22:21 ESV**

"Every day means something, nothing just happens. Everything falls under the sovereignty of God. He allows what he chooses to allow. Each day is prophetic and purposed. So write what happened and let's see Gods sovereignty in action." - +DRJIV

Day 1

One means: The number of Wholeness and Unity

Today you must work towards being whole. You must look within yourself and be unified with God and his will for your life. Be honest about what and who broke you. Take this day to address it and bring closure.

Focus Scripture: 1 Peter 3:8

Day 2

Two means: The number of covenant.

Today you must work towards identifying good covenant and worthless covenant. Be careful that you are not still tied to people, places, or things for fear of being alone.

Focus Scripture: Romans 8:31

Day 3

Three means: The number of the Godhead

You have Never been in this alone.

Focus Scripture: Ecclesiastes 4:12

Day 4

Four means: The number of world impact by way of the four corners of the earth

Today you must influence, impact, impart, and dominate

Focus Scripture: Romans 8:19

Day 5

Five means: Grace manifested

Today you must understand that you have been given as much power and more to counter act the powers that are working to frustrate your life. Work your grace.

Focus Scripture: Ephesians 4:7

Day 6

Six means: The number of flesh and humanity

Today understand your humanity, your responsibility, and your reward. In spite of a possible fall because of your humanity understand you have something greater than the fall, redemption.

Focus Scripture: Genesis 1:27

____

____

____

____

Day 7

Seven means: Divine revolution and cycles

Today address the uncompleted cycles. Take time out today, sit down for 15min. and think about everything you started and never finished. Pick them back up and finish them. You still have time only 93 more days to go.

Focus Scripture: Psalm 138:8

____

____

____

____

Day 8

Eight means: New beginnings

Today, focus only on new things happening in your life. There are new connections, new opportunities, and new outcomes. Getup and look for new. Be proactive, because new wont just fall into your lap.

Isaiah 43:19

Day 9

Nine means: The number of reproduction, and the fullness of blessing

Today, your focus will be on being full. Everything in your life points to this moment where you are full, full of power, full of might, full of glory, full of love , and full of compassion. Be full, and be willing to reproduce so that others who are not can see you example and follow. Be full on purpose.

Focus Scripture: John 15:8

Day 10

Ten means: The number of God's divine law, and ways and measures

Today think about Gods divine law and boundaries he wants you to work in between. Not what man feels you should, or should not do. How does the father view me? Am I walking out His laws with the life He gave?

Focus Scripture: Romans 7:12

Day 11

Eleven means: The number of Paradigm shift

Today your realm of authority has shifted, and your life is now be orchestrated under a banner of power. Speak into atmospheres for what took years to complete will now take days.

Focus Scripture: 1 King 6:38

Day 12

Twelve means: The number of divine government and the apostle rule

Today I hear the father say new government with new rules that will produce new bounty. Walk in the will of God for that which concerns you is not only perfected but it has been so ordered by the government in which you have given your allegiance. The Kingdom of God.

Focus Scripture: Psalm 22:28, John 15:19, Romans 12:2

Day 13

Thirteen means: The number of revolt against divine law

Today, let's be very clear that you have an enemy who doesn't want you to complete this assignment let alone the assignment for your life, the very reason why you exist. Be careful what you let in your life, for you might be entertaining your assassin. It could be anyone, including you.

Focus Scripture: 2 Timothy 4: 3-5

____

____

____

____

Day 14

Fourteen means: The number of the New Creation

Today let the creative anointing of God rest on you. As you are a new creation, create something new. Today create new cycles which will bless you and everyone who is connected to you.

Focus Scripture: 2 Corinthians 5:17

____

____

____

____

Day 15

Fifteen means: The number of Levitical servant

Today find yourself in the temple service. Where ever you

attend as the place where you are feed spiritually, go serve and show your gratitude through your service. There is beauty in the service of God within His temple.

Focus Scripture: Psalm 27:4

Day 16

Sixteen means: Experiential Sanctification

Today you make it your business to live holy. To Experience what is means to be set apart and different, and really experience what it means to be a child of God.

Focus Scripture: 1 Peter 1:16

Day 17

Seventeen means: Lawlessness

Today I want you to defy the Law that been over your life that has kept you bound by fear, your past, spoken word curses, anxieties, or feeling that you are not good enough. Revolt against depression and against the lies you once believed about yourself.

Focus Scripture: Romans 12:2

Day 18

Eighteen means: Pillar

Today be someone's support, not their crutch. Allow God to lead you to be something to someone, even if you don't have that for yourself. Pray this prayer: God teach me how to be a pillar.

Focus Scripture: John 15:13

Day 19

Nineteen means: King, Royalty and Government

Today your focus is not just being royalty, or being a part of a royal priest hood, but it is exercising of the grace, authority, and wisdom of the office. You can't be royal in name only.

Focus Scripture: 1 Peter 2:9

Day 20

Twenty means: Going out and coming in, perfected waiting period.

Today before you demand relief or payment, or the blessing be sure you have meet all the qualifications.

Focus Scripture: Genesis 31: 38-42

Day 21

Twenty-0ne means: The great wickedness and rebellion and sin.

Today be honest with you. It has been your choices and your sin which has you facing the present conditions you are coming out of. Repent, for there is a way of escape.

Focus Scripture: 2 Corinthians 7:10

Day 22

Twenty-two means: disorder and chaos, cursing

Today you must focus on focusing. It's really easy to watch

great intentions become a huge catastrophic moment. When you allow what's around you to alter what God has given you; you stand to miss or lose more than just your moment.

Focus Scripture: Song of Solomon 2:15

____
____
____
____

Day 23

Twenty- three means: Cursing turned into a blessing, a spiritual uptrend

Today rejoice for he has turned your curse to a blessing.

Focus Scripture: Joel 2:25

____
____
____
____

Day 24

Twenty-four means: Elders of Israel, Strategy, Priesthood, (God's Power and Authority, and perfect foundation) and the Worship of God

Today God has an order and a strategy for you; In order to find it you must create the perfect foundation for any strategy which is worship. Order + Strategy = Success

Focus Scripture: Jeremiah 31:36

Day 25

Twenty-five means: Grace upon Grace and the Sovereignty of God

Today the focus is on giving to others what you might one day need. Extend Grace upon grace so that you can get grace upon grace.

Focus Scripture: Luke 6:38

Day 26

Twenty-six means: Political, and Politicians

Today praying for our governmental officials are important. How they govern affects all of us. Favor and influence is important for where you are headed, so pray for it.

Focus Scripture: 1 Timothy 2: 1-3

Day 27

Twenty-seven means: Horn, the phrase mercy seat and candle sticks appears 27 times

Today represent God. In all that you do point to him, the sacrifice he made with is son and his heart to redeem. Show mercy today, and much of it.

Focus Scripture: Romans 12:16

Day 28

Twenty-eight means: Fortress, and Strong Hold

Today you must build one up and tear one down. A strong hold can be a good thing if it keeps you in line and the enemy out. However is the stronghold in which you find yourself in keeps you stuck, depressed, and outside of God's will tear it down. Only that which is from God and for God can bring you the success of God.

Focus Scripture: 2 Corinthians 10:4

Day 29

Twenty-nine means: Victory over Edom, (Laws of Establishment Victory)

Today is very clear without any hesitation to drive forward. There is a law that is written over you, it is the law of victory. You can't lose. Purse, Conquer, and Rule.

Focus Scripture: 1 Corinthians 15:57

____

____

____

____

Day 30

Thirty means: The number of priest's maturity

Today allow God's way and his device he chooses to use mature you. He often uses what you least expect, and what you least expect often times is exactly what you needed.

Focus Scripture: 2 Samuel 5:4

____

____

____

____

Day 31

Thirty-one means: Hebrew name of God *EL* is made up of 2 words lamed representing 30 and Aleph representing 1

Today let El get the Glory. Allow nothing else to stand with him or even in His shadow.

Focus Scripture: Exodus 20:3

Day 32

Thirty-two means: Conspiracy

Today, watch out for those that always speak well of you and can never tell you the truth about yourself. They are hoping it's the truth that will destroy you, and be certain they are ready to take you place. I hear God say, "Clean up the mess you made."

Focus Scripture: Micah 2:1

Day 33

Thirty-three means: Purification of the Holy Spirit

Today I clearly hear, all of your efforts will fail without the leading of the Holy Spirit. You must be careful to synchronize every patter and step with Him. Talk to Him before you act.

Focus Scripture: Romans 8:14

Day 34

Thirty-four means: Division

Today pray against any divisive spirit, and anything that would separate you from your primary purpose and goal. Rebuke the devil and he will flee.

Focus Scripture: 1 Corinthians 1:10

Day 35

Thirty-five means: Rest from Enemies

Today, decree and declare every enemy that has tried to assassinate your character, your family, and your purpose will cease from troubling you and everything that is assigned to you to frustrate and kill you, rewrite the assignment, that nothing will come neigh you.

Focus Scripture: Joshua 21:44,45

Day 36

Thirty-six means: AI, shooting yourself in the foot.

Today don't allow the people in your camp to cause you to fall into the hands of an angry God, and you miss what he has destined for you. Rather, train, and take those with you and go up and attack, for this day the Lord has delivered the victory into your hands.

Focus Scripture: Joshua chapters 7, 8

____

____

____

____

Day 37

Thirty-seven means: Warrior

Today you are to fight with integrity and intensity. The battle belongs to the Lord, but he is using your hands. Fight well.

Focus Scripture: 2 Samuel 10:12

____

____

____

____

Day 38

Thirty-eight means: Death in the Wilderness

Today you must understand that complaints and those that bring them with no solutions are not a part of the solution. Understand that their death, one by one, in your life which doesn't mean it will be a physical one, but a season of being cut off from you, which is a necessity. The Promised Land awaits you.

Focus Scripture: Joshua 5:6

Day 39

Thirty-nine means: The Amount of Lashes Jesus took

Today let's be really clear, the only reason why we have this opportunity to be greater than we have ever been is because of Jesus. Let him into your heart today, again or maybe for the first time. For he desires to be Lord over your Life. Today Give up the crown, and place it on Him.

Focus Scripture: John 14:12

Day 40

Forty means: The number of spiritual preparation through trials and wilderness, and Maximum Divine Discipline

There is an adage, "You can take the horse to water but you can't make him drink." Discipline goes beyond don't do this or that, It is about knowing when to do, and being disciplined enough to wait on the proper season, timing, and resources to be in place. So when you make you move you will see success.

Focus Scripture: Hebrews 12:11

Day 41

Forty-one means: To misunderstand or be deceived (the flow of time)

Today be sure that what you heard is what God said.

Focus Scripture: Philippians 4:6-7

Day 42

Forty-two means: The generations in which Christ came down through.

You life is the response to a generations cry. You are here because God's remedy for the generation is you. Today you must be what you were sent here to be.

Focus Scripture: 2 Peter 1:20-21

Day 43

Forty-three means: Resurrection and being Restored

Today have some life about you. He has revived, resurrected, and restored everything that concerns you.

Focus Scripture: Revelation 21:5

Day 44

Forty-four means: Warning to obey God

Let's be very clear your very survival depends on what comes out of His mouth. Don't give up everything you have worked so hard to create because you won't listen to His word.

Focus Scripture: Deuteronomy 8:18

Day 45

Forty-five means: Provision, Protection, and Preservation. You will truly recognize that He is the Lord.

It's often times hard to recognize the awesome power of God. In our human frailty we often mistake His power with our works and our works with His Power. Get to know him, and recognize God not you acting as god, but really Him. This is one of those God let me see you face moments.

Focus Scripture: Exodus 33:18

Day 46

Forty-six means: Those who have chosen to serve the Lord, and Pregnancy

What do you have in? Today you will make a lot of choices but remember you choices will affect what you are carrying inside of you. Whether you choose to give birth, delay its birthing, or kill it while you are still carrying it. The choice is yours.

Focus Scripture: John 15:16

Day 47

Forty-seven means: Separating the clean from the unclean, Peace

Have you ever sat in a dirty house, or dirty room and just

couldn't think or bring your thoughts together? All the clutter and dirt messed with your head. Well today Get Up and Clean Up. You say you want peace but you are so willing to get relaxed in the storm, and even create your own disastrous waves. Get Up and clean your life up that you may have peace.

Focus Scripture: 1Timothy 6: 3-5

____

____

____

____

Day 48

Forty-one means: Knowing Seeing Experiencing God, Given an Inheritance or a dwelling place.

There is truly a nomadic spirit afoot. Causing people to roam and be unfocused, and deliberate in not setting down roots. Not having an inheritance is a curse; even the *priest inheritance was the Lord.*

Focus Scripture: Psalm 1:1-6

____

____

____

____

Day 49

Forty-nine means: The Day before Jubilee happens

I hear the spirit of the Lord say this is a day of dreams, a day of seeing the release right before it is released. For the Lord as certainly called your dreams into reality and His provision sits with it. Do not be afraid to announce it and walk in it. For tomorrow is your Jubilee.

Focus Scripture: Jeremiah 23:28

Day 50

Fifty means: Jubilee and a time of forgiving all debts.

Oh my goodness, It's finally hear the day that every debt against your life has been canceled. Not just money, but even what we owed but never gave. Fresh start begins today.

Focus Scripture: Leviticus 25:11-12

Are you excited!!!!!! For the first 50days I gave you the meaning and I gave you my insight on the day, but now it's your turn. Take the next 50days to put in your insight. The Focus Scripture will still be provided on all but 1, The Father will Lead You on the Scripture that pertains to you specifically. Now let's get to work.

Day 51

Fifty-one means: Sanctification

Today my focus is on:

Focus Scripture: 2 Timothy 2:21

Day 52

Fifty-two means: Corruption, bringing down walls

Today my focus is on:

Focus Scripture: Joshua 6:20

Day 53

Fifty-three means: The Glory of God, and Entering into the Kingdom. A great catch, large fish

Today my focus is on:

Focus Scripture: 1 Corinthians 4:20

Day 54

Fifty-four means: Learning and realizing who God is, the security of the believer, and Redemption.

Today my focus is on:

Focus Scripture: Philippians 1:6

Day 55

Fifty-five means: Double Portion of Grace

Today my focus is on:

Focus Scripture: James 1:5

Day 56

Fifty-six means: To Awake from Sleep

Today my focus is on:

Focus Scripture: Isaiah 52:1

Day 57

Fifty-seven means: means gift and honor

Today my focus is on:

Focus Scripture: 1 Samuel 2:30

Day 58

Fifty-eight means: God ensures we know him, and you will know the Lord. To weep

Today my focus is on:

Focus Scripture: Colossians 3:18

Day 59

Fifty-nine means: God is a Jealous God

Today my focus is on:

Focus Scripture: Deuteronomy 4:24

Day 60

Sixty means: Pride

Today my focus is on:

Focus Scripture: Proverbs 16:5

Day 61

Sixty-one means: Paying what is owed, Income Tax

Today my focus is on:

Focus Scripture: Matthew 22:21

Day 62

Sixty-two means: The End

Today my focus is on:

Focus Scripture: Matthew 24:13

Day 63

Sixty-three means: Israel (Chosen People)

Today my focus is on:

Focus Scripture: 1 Peter 2:9

Day 64

Sixty-four means: Manifestation of the Sons of God

Today my focus is on:

Focus Scripture: Romans 8:14

Day 65

Sixty-five means: Glory

Today my focus is on:

Focus Scripture: 1 Corinthians 10:31

Day 66

Sixty-six means: Worldliness, False Worship

Today my focus is on:

Focus Scripture: Colossians 3:5

Day 67

Sixty-seven means: Giving

Today my focus is on:

Focus Scripture: 2 Corinthians 9:7

Day 68

Sixty-eight means: Serving in the World

Today my focus is on:

Focus Scripture: Matthew 5:13

Day 69

Sixty-nine means: Running the course

Today my focus is on:

____

____

____

Focus Scripture: Colossians 1:10

____

____

____

____

Day 70

Seventy means: Elders, Prophets, Restoration, and Atonement

Today my focus is on:

____

____

____

Focus Scripture: Jeremiah 30:17

____

____

____

____

____

Day 71

Seventy-one means: Strait (a narrow passage of water

connecting two sea or two large areas of water)

Today my focus is on:

Focus Scripture: John 7:38

Day 72

Seventy-two means: Gatekeeper, guard, security

Today my focus is on:

Focus Scripture: John 10:1-42

Day 73

Seventy-three means: Freedom

Today my focus is on:

Focus Scripture: 1Peter 2:16

Day 74

Seventy-four means: Spiritual Freedom

Today my focus is on:

Focus Scripture: John 8:31-36

Day 75

Seventy-five means: Sovereign Plan

Today my focus is on:

Focus Scripture: Genesis 12:4

Day 76

Seventy-six means: Skill

Today my focus is on:

Focus Scripture: Exodus 35:31

Day 77

Seventy-seven means: Vengeance

Today my focus is on:

Focus Scripture: Romans 12:19

Day 78

Seventy-eight means: Process of becoming Godly

Today my focus is on:

Focus Scripture: Ephesians 4:14

Day 79

Seventy-nine means: Hardness of Heart

Today my focus is on:

Focus Scripture: Mark 8:17

Day 80

Eighty means: Strength

Today my focus is on:

Focus Scripture: Deuteronomy 31:6

Day 81

Eighty-one means: Grace Counter attack

Today my focus is on:

Focus Scripture: Ephesians 6:13-21

Day 82

Eighty-two means: Breakpoint; break with the past

Today my focus is on:

Focus Scripture: Psalm 147 15-18

Day 83

Eighty-three means: High Priest

Today my focus is on:

Focus Scripture: Hebrews 4:15

Day 84

Eighty-four means: Weakness of the Church (meet the churches need)

Today my focus is on:

Focus Scripture: Haggai 1:4

Day 85

Eighty-five means: Eye (Spy out)

Today my focus is on:

Focus Scripture: Joshua 14:10

Day 86

Eighty-six means: Legalistic Persecution

Today my focus is on:

Focus Scripture: Matthew 6:1-2

Day 87

Eighty-seven means: Donkey, or mule (transportation system)

Today my focus is on:

Focus Scripture: Numbers 22:22-31

Day 88

Eighty-eight means: Blessing

Today my focus is on:

Focus Scripture: ________________ You Find The Scripture

Day 89

Eighty-nine means: Without Divine Authority

Today my focus is on:

____

____

____

Focus Scripture: 2Kings 5:20-27

____

____

____

____

Day 90

Ninety means: New Order

Today my focus is on:

____

____

____

Focus Scripture: Romans 12:2

____

____

____

____

Day 91

Ninety-one means: Emergency

Today my focus is on:

Focus Scripture: Philippians 4:6-9

Day 92

Ninety-two means: Servant hood

Today my focus is on:

Focus Scripture: Luke 22:27

Day 93

Ninety-three means: Guilt

Today my focus is on:

Focus Scripture: Romans 8:1

Day 94

Ninety-four means: Footstool

Today my focus is on:

Focus Scripture: Luke20: 42-43

Day 95

Ninety-five means: Hero

Today my focus is on:

Focus Scripture: Philippians 4:8-9

Day 96

Ninety-six means: Spoils of Victory

Today my focus is on:

Focus Scripture: Hebrews 7:1-28

Day 97

Ninety-seven means: Reduction in Force

Today my focus is on:

Focus Scripture: Judges 7

Day 98

Ninety-eight means: Ichabod (the Glory of the Lord has departed)

Today my focus is on:

Focus Scripture: 1 Samuel 4:21-22

Day 99

Ninety-nine means: The Challenger (almost but not quite)

Today my focus is on:

Focus Scripture: Psalm 72:2-17

Day 100

One hundred means: Maximum Divine Good Production,

Multiplier, Liberty, and Promise Attained

Today my focus is on:

____

____

____

Focus Scripture: Genesis 26:12, Deuteronomy 1:11

____

____

____

____

You Have Gone Full 100 days. I know this process hasn't been easy and I know you have had to fight all the way through it. But, you made it. It is not how you started this race but it is that you finished, and accomplished something. This is only the beginning. Thank you for taking this opportunity to make **In 100 Day or Less** apart of your life.

Which Day Will You Never Forget? ___________________

Why?

____

____

____

____

____

____

2 THE PLAN

100 Days or Less Challenge

Welcome to **ThePlan** section of In 100 days or Less. This is a New season of your life. I, like you, am totally excited about everything that is about to happen. I feel such an anticiapation of greatness and great things, and I for one am not letting this time run out, or this moment to leave without my active participation. This section that God has released me to create is your road map, your tracking tool, your auxilary bible. It will help you address areas in your life that you have been stuck in, and force you out of that stuck place. You will disarm fear, and propel into a life of Faith with Works. "I am just excited that we get an opportunity to take this journey together. Are you ready? Well Let's Go!" - +DRJIV

Mediate on these scripture while working toward accomplishing these Goals:

Proverbs 16:1
Proverbs 16:9
Proverbs 19:21
James 2: 14-26

First Things First

List Your Five Major Goal You Will Accomplish.

GOAL 1.

The Plan To Accomplish: (The how to do may change but the *Goal* will never change) Remember it may not take you 100days to finish it. Keep track of the days.

The Accountabilty Partner chosen for this ***Goal*** is:

10 Day Progress:

20 Day Progress:

30 Day Progress:

Its been 30 days Now, How do you feel about this Goal? Even if its No Longer important to you still finish it out. You might be surprised to know that you only lost interest because of the warefare, it was selfish to being with, or you just wasn't ready for the commitment. Still Finish.

Your Comments

Your Accountability Partner Comments

The Next 20 Day Progress:

The Next 20 Day Progress:

____
____
____
____
____

The Next 20 Day Progress:

____
____
____
____
____

Only 10 More Left. You can do this.
Zephaniah 3:19 Behold, at that time I will undo all that afflict thee; and I will save her that is halt, and gather her that was driven out; and I will get them praise and fame in every land where they have been put to shame.KJV

Final 10 days:

____
____
____
____
____

Date Goal Completed: ______________
How many did it take you to complete your goal?

____

GOAL 2.

The Plan To Accomplish: (The how to do may change but the *Goal* will never change) Remember it may not take you 100days to finish it. Keep track of the days.

The Accountabilty Partner chosen for this ***Goal*** is:

10 Day Progress:

20 Day Progress:

30 Day Progress:

Its been 30 days Now, How do you feel about this Goal? Even if its No Longer important to you still finish it out. You might be surprised to know that you only lost interest because of the warefare, it was selfish to being with, or you just wasn't ready for the commitment. Still Finish.

Your Comments

Your Accountability Partner Comments

The Next 20 Day Progress:

The Next 20 Day Progress:

____

____

The Next 20 Day Progress:

____

____

____

____

____

Only 10 More Left. You can do this.
Zephaniah 3:19 Behold, at that time I will undo all that afflict thee; and I will save her that is halt, and gather her that was driven out; and I will get them praise and fame in every land where they have been put to shame.KJV

Final 10 days:

____

____

____

____

____

Date Goal Completed: ________________
How many did it take you to complete your goal?

____

GOAL 3.

The Plan To Accomplish: (The how to do may change but the *Goal* will never change) Remember it may not take you 100days to finish it. Keep track of the days.

____

____

____

____

____

____

____

____

____

The Accountabilty Partner chosen for this ***Goal*** is:

____

10 Day Progress:

____

____

____

____

____

20 Day Progress:

____

____

____

____

____

30 Day Progress:

____

____

____

____

____

Its been 30 days Now, How do you feel about this Goal? Even if its No Longer important to you still finish it out. You might be surprised to know that you only lost interest because of the warefare, it was selfish to being with, or you just wasn't ready for the commitment. Still Finish.

Your Comments

Your Accountability Partner Comments

The Next 20 Day Progress:

The Next 20 Day Progress:

The Next 20 Day Progress:

Only 10 More Left. You can do this.

Zephaniah 3:19 Behold, at that time I will undo all that afflict thee; and I will save her that is halt, and gather her that was driven out; and I will get them praise and fame in every land where they have been put to shame.KJV

Final 10 days:

Date Goal Completed: ________________

How many did it take you to complete your goal?

____

GOAL 4.

The Plan To Accomplish: (The how to do may change but the *Goal* will never change) Remember it may not take you 100days to finish it. Keep track of the days.

The Accountabilty Partner chosen for this ***Goal*** is:

10 Day Progress:

20 Day Progress:

30 Day Progress:

Its been 30 days Now, How do you feel about this Goal? Even if its No Longer important to you still finish it out. You might be surprised to know that you only lost interest because of the warefare, it was selfish to being with, or you just wasn't ready for the commitment. Still Finish.

Your Comments

Your Accountability Partner Comments

The Next 20 Day Progress:

The Next 20 Day Progress:

The Next 20 Day Progress:

Only 10 More Left. You can do this.
Zephaniah 3:19 Behold, at that time I will undo all that afflict thee; and I will save her that is halt, and gather her that was driven out; and I will get them praise and fame in every land where they have been put to shame.KJV

Final 10 days:

____

____

____

____

____

Date Goal Completed: ______________
How many did it take you to complete your goal?

____

GOAL 5.

The Plan To Accomplish: (The how to do may change but the *Goal* will never change) Remember it may not take you 100days to finish it. Keep track of the days.

____

____

____

____

____

____

____

____

____

The Accountabilty Partner chosen for this ***Goal*** is:

____

10 Day Progress:

____
____
____
____
____

20 Day Progress:

____
____
____
____
____

30 Day Progress:

____
____
____
____
____

Its been 30 days Now, How do you feel about this Goal? Even if its No Longer important to you still finish it out. You might be surprised to know that you only lost interest because of the warefare, it was selfish to being with, or you just wasn't ready for the commitment. Still Finish.

Your Comments

____
____
____
____
____

Your Accountability Partner Comments

____

____

____

____

____

The Next 20 Day Progress:

____

____

____

____

____

The Next 20 Day Progress:

____

____

____

____

____

The Next 20 Day Progress:

____

____

____

____

____

Only 10 More Left. You can do this.

Zephaniah 3:19 Behold, at that time I will undo all that afflict thee; and I will save her that is halt, and gather her that was driven out; and I will get them praise and fame in every land where they have been put to shame.KJV

Final 10 days:

____
____
____
____
____

Date Goal Completed: ________________
How many did it take you to complete your goal?
____

3 DAILY CHARTING THECOURSE

Daily Charting The Course

You're blessed when you stay on course, walking steadily on the road revealed only by God, and not the opinion of people. You're blessed when you follow his directions, and doing your best to find him in everything. That's right, you don't go off on your own; you walk straight along the road he set in place. God prescribed the right way to live and he expects us to live it. Your prayer should be, Father let my steps be steady, sure, keeping to the course you set; then I will never compare my life with anyone else's. He will speak straight from his heart to yours. Learn the pattern of his ways. Do what he tell you and you can't help but win.

Daily Charting Focus: Psalm 119: 1-8

____

____

____

____

____

____

"I know exactly what it is like when you get started on something and you just have other things to happen that try and stop you, or they may not utterly stop, but they have just enough of your attention to distract you. Well not this time.

This time, everyday you will chart what you do and you will Finish your Goals." - +DRJIV

WEEK 1

Write in your Goals and Place a Check Mark
If You Worked Toward Your Goals

GOALS	MON	TUE	WED	THUR	FRI	SAT	SUN
1.							
2.							
3.							
4.							
5.							

WEEK 2

Write in your Goals and Place a Check Mark
If You Worked Toward Your Goals

GOALS	MON	TUE	WED	THUR	FRI	SAT	SUN
1.							
2.							
3.							
4.							
5.							

WEEK 3

Write in your Goals and Place a Check Mark
If You Worked Toward Your Goals

GOALS	MON	TUE	WED	THUR	FRI	SAT	SUN
1.							
2.							
3.							
4.							
5.							

WEEK 4

Write in your Goals and Place a Check Mark
If You Worked Toward Your Goals

GOALS	MON	TUE	WED	THUR	FRI	SAT	SUN
1.							
2.							
3.							
4.							
5.							

WEEK 5

Write in your Goals and Place a Check Mark
If You Worked Toward Your Goals

GOALS	MON	TUE	WED	THUR	FRI	SAT	SUN
1.							
2.							
3.							
4.							
5.							

WEEK 6

Write in your Goals and Place a Check Mark
If You Worked Toward Your Goals

GOALS	MON	TUE	WED	THUR	FRI	SAT	SUN
1.							
2.							
3.							
4.							
5.							

WEEK 7

Write in your Goals and Place a Check Mark
If You Worked Toward Your Goals

GOALS	MON	TUE	WED	THUR	FRI	SAT	SUN
1.							
2.							
3.							
4.							
5.							

WEEK 8

Write in your Goals and Place a Check Mark
If You Worked Toward Your Goals

GOALS	MON	TUE	WED	THUR	FRI	SAT	SUN
1.							
2.							
3.							
4.							
5.							

WEEK 9

Write in your Goals and Place a Check Mark
If You Worked Toward Your Goals

GOALS	MON	TUE	WED	THUR	FRI	SAT	SUN
1.							
2.							
3.							
4.							
5.							

WEEK 10

Write in your Goals and Place a Check Mark
If You Worked Toward Your Goals

GOALS	MON	TUE	WED	THUR	FRI	SAT	SUN
1.							
2.							
3.							
4.							
5.							

WEEK 11

Write in your Goals and Place a Check Mark
If You Worked Toward Your Goals

GOALS	MON	TUE	WED	THUR	FRI	SAT	SUN
1.							
2.							
3.							
4.							
5.							

WEEK 12

Write in your Goals and Place a Check Mark
If You Worked Toward Your Goals

GOALS	MON	TUE	WED	THUR	FRI	SAT	SUN
1.							
2.							
3.							
4.							
5.							

WEEK 13

Write in your Goals and Place a Check Mark
If You Worked Toward Your Goals

GOALS	MON	TUE	WED	THUR	FRI	SAT	SUN
1.							
2.							
3.							
4.							
5.							

WEEK 14

Write in your Goals and Place a Check Mark
If You Worked Toward Your Goals

GOALS	MON	TUE	WED	THUR	FRI	SAT	SUN
1.							
2.							
3.							
4.							
5.							

WEEK 15

Write in your Goals and Place a Check Mark
If You Worked Toward Your Goals

GOALS	MON	TUE	WED	THUR	FRI	SAT	SUN
1.							
2.							
3.							
4.							
5.							

ABOUT THE AUTHOR

Bishop J. Isaac Vaughn is the Founder Impact Life Worship Center, Charlotte, NC. This man of God is a uniquely anointed "Out of the Box" type of leader whose heart is after God. Totally submitted to the mandate God has placed upon his life, Bishop Vaughn is one who fully understands the importance of the Apostolic and Prophetic Ministries, in full operation, in the present day church to produce Kingdom results, as well as the full acceptance and operation of the five-fold ministry. The global mandate that God has place on this Apostle's life is to be a Bridge and People Builder. Instructing Sons and Daughters, and those given to him for seasons in the ways of God; providing practical teaching in areas of lack, releasing them in areas where there is frustration, prophesying the Heart and Mind of God toward them, preparing them so their legitimacy doesn't come into question, and being an example of how to surrender to God's process through the work of the Holy Spirit.

Bishop Vaughn has been privileged to proclaim the good news of Jesus Christ around the country, and overseas at various ministries, universities, civic events, and conferences as a speaker and lecturer. Bishop Vaughn has held several professional licenses in the field of Banking and Finance, and understands a part of his Mandate is to help bring Financial Stability, Administrative Insight and Economic Empowerment to Pastors, Para-Ministries, Churches, and Congregations around the World.

Made in the USA
Columbia, SC
07 March 2021

33489044R00050